I dedicate this book to my beautiful da

Sophia Rose Blum

Story written by Dr. Elisa Shipon-Blum

Illustrated by Diane Salus

Copyright@ 2003 Rev. 2009 by Dr. Elisa Shipon-Blum and Selective Mutism Anxiety Research and Treatment Center
SMart-Center Philadelphia, Pennsylvania
All Rights Reserved. Reproduction in whole or in part without written permission
From Dr. Elisa Shipon-Blum is prohibited

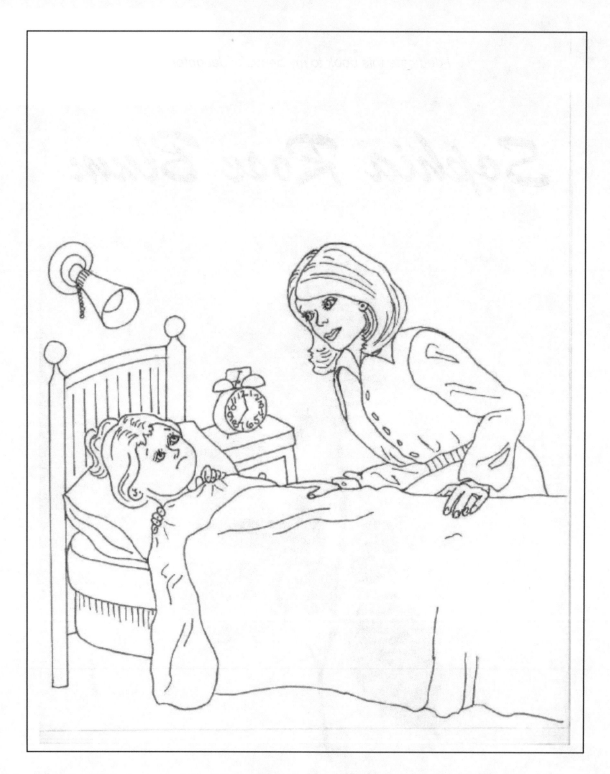

    At 7 am, Katie's alarm clock went off, but like every morning, Katie stayed in bed until Mom came into her room.
    "Katie? Honey, come on, get up sweetie, you need to get up and dressed!"
    "But, Mommy, I am tired, and my head and tummy hurt again today. I don't think I can go to school," said Katie.
    Mom checked Katie over to be sure she was not ill. She gave Katie an extra special hug and kiss.
    "Katie, you feel this way many mornings, and you will be fine."
    "I guess so, Mommy," Katie said.

    Making up a game to help Katie get dressed, Mom said, "Ok, Katie, I am going to count to 50. If you can get up, dressed, with your teeth brushed and into the kitchen in less than 50 seconds, I will give you an extra sticker for your chart!"

    "Really," exclaimed Katie.

    Katie immediately jumped out of bed, grabbing her clothes that she and mom set out the night before.

    "Ok, ready set go…1, 2, 3," said Mom.

Mom counted very slowly as she happily watched Katie getting dressed so swiftly.

    "…. 32, 33, 34…"

    At this point, Katie was dressed, her shoes on and teeth just about brushed! Mom watched, realizing that Katie was feeling better already. She obviously wanted an extra sticker on her chart.

    "…. 44, 45, 46…"

"DONE AND READY, MOMMY!" Katie excitedly yelled, as she was about to sit at the table, ready for breakfast!

"Wow Katie, you certainly were fast today! I am proud of you!"

Katie smiled, kicking her feet excitedly as she stared at the stickers mom showed her.

"Well, Katie, which one do you want?"

"Oh, that one Mommy! Look, I only need two more until I get five. Then we can go to the store to get a reward! YEHHHHHH," exclaimed Katie.

Katie placed the sticker right under the last one, and just jumped up and down excitedly.

"Ok, honey, let's eat breakfast."

Katie managed to eat breakfast, sitting happily and contentedly as she thought about her sticker chart and what she might get when she reached five stickers.

"OK, Katie, bus is here, come on, let's get out there…"

As soon as Mom said this, Katie's complete facial expression changed. She slowly got up, got her coat on, and went out to the bus as her mom lead her. Katie felt a sharp pang in her tummy.

"I don't like this feeling," thought Katie.

    Katie kissed her mom, and then walked to her seat on the bus with her head down and her face showing no emotions. Mom watched as Katie sat alone, just like she did on other mornings.
    The bus, filled with other kids laughing and talking among each other, was not a place where Katie wanted to be.
    Katie wanted so badly to talk and laugh with the other children, but she just couldn't seem to do it. The thought of talking or even whispering to the other kids made Katie feel scared.
    Katie grabbed her tummy as she felt a pang of discomfort, and she sat quietly and alone for the remainder of the bus ride.

    When the bus arrived at school, Katie walked directly to her classroom.
    A few kids bumped into her, but Katie did not acknowledge them when one of the little boys apologized. Katie just kept walking…. alone.
    She did not mean to ignore the other children. She was thinking about being called on during show and tell and the thought of having to answer a question in class made her feel very nervous.

Inside the classroom, Katie stood next to Mrs. Ryan's desk as the other kids ran around the class and laughed at a show and tell project that one of the little girls brought in for that day.

"Come look at the special magic trick that Connie brought to school, Katie," said Mrs. Ryan, Katie's teacher.

However, Katie just stood in the same spot, twisting her brown braids and feeling scared. She had no expression on her face and just looked down at the floor.

Mrs. Ryan came over and took Katie's hand, leading her to the group of children sitting on the floor.

"Come on Katie, I want you to see this, "Mrs. Ryan said quietly to Katie, giving her a gentle pat on her head and taking her hand. She led Katie to the circle where the children were patiently waiting to start show and tell.

    Katie watched as all the children played with the magic trick.

    "Ok," said Mrs. Ryan. "I want everyone to take a turn and tell me how this trick works. OK, Sam, you start!"

    One by one, all the kids guessed at the secret of how the magic trick worked. When it was Katie's turn, she just sat there, staring at the ground.

    "Mrs. Ryan, Katie doesn't talk. She can't tell us anything," said Billy.

    "Katie most certainly does talk Billy! She just has a 'hard time getting out her words right now…Everyone has something that is hard or scary to do," said Mrs. Ryan as she winked and smiled at Katie.

    Since Katie seemed relaxed, Mrs. Ryan asked Katie if she knew how to perform the trick. Katie nodded. Mrs. Ryan sensed that Katie wanted to try the magic trick.

    "Okay, then take the magic trick Katie, and show the class just how Connie performed it," said Mrs. Ryan.

At first, Katie hesitated, but then, she slowly took the trick from Mrs. Ryan. Katie took her time, but she performed the trick just how Connie had.

"Great job, Katie," exclaimed Mrs. Ryan. "I am super proud of you!"

All the other kids in the class smiled and seemed proud of Katie as well. Katie felt proud too. She seemed happy and smiled as she looked at Mrs. Ryan. Mrs. Ryan was very pleased at how relaxed Katie seemed right now.

"This wasn't so scary," thought Katie.

Right before recess, all the kids ran to the door in anticipation of playing outside. Katie lined up, but she did not have a smile on her face. Recess was one of the hardest times of the day for Katie. She would much rather stay inside and draw or do puzzles then to go on the playground with all the other children.

    Katie often sat alone or played on the swings as all the kids ran around, laughing and chasing each other.

    "Katie," yelled Emma. "Come play with us today!"

    Katie looked over at Emma but did not say a word as she continued to walk over to the swings. She wanted to play with the other girls, especially Emma…. But she just couldn't. She couldn't even look in their direction. She felt a funny feeling in her tummy and just kept walking.

    For the rest of recess, Katie was on the swings. She liked the swings the best. Sometimes other kids would swing next to her and she felt included in their swinging games.

During the afternoon reading time, most of the kids had to read to the teacher. When it was Katie's turn, she just stood there, looking down at the book.

"Did you like the book, Katie," asked Mrs. Ryan.

Katie nodded.

"Good. Now, I want you to show me the part in the book where Mrs. Clark had to drive her baby to the doctor."

Katie took the book and easily pointed to the third page, right where Mrs. Ryan was talking about.

"Great Katie, you certainly answered that very fast," exclaimed Mrs. Ryan.

Mrs. Ryan was very proud of Katie's efforts.

Katie felt proud of herself too! She really liked Mrs. Ryan and enjoyed being with her. She looked forward to her time alone with Mrs. Ryan and felt much less scared with her than she did in the beginning of the school year.

It was much easier to do her reading activities when she and Mrs. Ryan were alone and away from the other group of kids. Sometimes Emma would join them for reading and that was something Katie looked forward too!

At 3 o'clock, Katie's mom came to pick her up. Katie ran over and gave her mom a great big hug. Mom tried to come into the classroom after school as much as possible.

Katie certainly enjoyed when she came to visit. When Mom was in school Katie felt much more comfortable and less scared. Plus, when Mom was in school, it gave Katie a chance to show her mom all the things she loved to do.

"How was school, honey," asked Mom, when all the kids and Mrs. Ryan were leaving to go home.
Katie tried to answer Mom, but could not seem to get the words out, which was very frustrating to Katie. Finally, when it was just Mom and Katie in the room, Katie was able to answer her mom.

"School was good today, Mommy. I pointed to parts in the book for Mrs. Ryan and it was easy. I hardly felt scared at all," said Katie.

"That is great, Katie," said Mom. "Tell me who brought show and tell in today?"

"Connie brought a great magic trick, and Mrs. Ryan let me show the class how the trick worked," whispered Katie.

"Katie, I cannot hear you, what did you say?" Asked Mom.
Katie spoke louder, repeating what Mom had asked her.

"I was so happy Mommy!"

"Oh, that is great, Katie. I am proud of you!" Mom gave Katie a super big hug and kiss "Mrs. Ryan was proud of me too, Mommy!" exclaimed Katie.

"Well, I think your efforts deserve a special sticker. What do you think of that idea?" asked Mom.

"Oh yes, Mommy, that would be great!"

Mom realized that Katie was practically yelling when she spoke.

Mom and Katie talked a bit in class, and then they went to the art room, so that Katie could show her Mom her new artwork. On the way, Mom asked Katie many questions as they walked hand in hand.
Katie answered Mom without much hesitation.
"This is wonderful progress," thought Mom. Just a few weeks ago, Katie could not speak at all in the hallways or classroom.

    On the way home from school, they stopped by Emma's house to pick her up. Emma came running to the car.

        "Hi Katie, I was waiting for you! I want to show you my new doll!" said Emma.

        "Wow Emma, your doll is cool! I love the pink dress and blue sparkled hair band."

        "Me too," laughed Emma. "It looks like the pink dress you wore for Halloween."

        "Yes, you are right, but my dress was much bigger," Katie said while laughing.

    Katie and Emma laughed and played for the rest of the afternoon. Mom enjoyed watching Katie so relaxed and having fun with her friend.

During dinner that evening, Katie told her parents and older brother about the magic trick that she performed at school.

"It was fun. Can I get more magic tricks at the store?" asked Katie.

"Sure sweetie. A few magic tricks may be a perfect reward for getting five stickers," said Mom.

"I know the perfect store to go to," said Dad. "It is right by Dr. Elwood's office, so after your appointment on Friday, we can certainly go get some more tricks."

"Oh goodie, I only need one more, so it will be easy," said Katie.

Mom and Dad looked at each other and smiled, they were so proud of Katie's enthusiasm.

After dinner, Katie colored her most recent masterpiece.

"Katie, your picture is beautiful, but you are going to have to finish it in the morning. It is just about time for bed. Five more minutes," said Mom.

She put out a timer and told Katie that if she went upstairs before it went off, she would receive her final sticker.

Katie heard what her mommy said and immediately put away her artwork and ran upstairs!

"WOW, Katie, I am impressed," said Mom.

"Well, the last three nights I did not come up in time, and I did not get my sticker, and I want my sticker! I can't wait to get some magic tricks!" said Katie, as she practically flew up the stairs!

"Well, you earned it sweetie. Get in your pajamas and let's spend some time together," said Mom, as she watched Katie running to her room.

This was one of Katie's favorite times of the day. She loved 'bedtime snuggle time'.
As Katie and Mom snuggled close, Mom listened to Katie talk about her feelings and thoughts.
"I was upset when Billy told Mrs. Ryan I don't talk, because I do talk! I just can't talk in school," said Katie.
"Did it hurt your feelings," asked Mom.
"Yes, kind of. People just don't understand me Mommy. No one really does," said Katie.
"We understand Katie, and so does Dr. Elwood and Mrs. Ryan," said Mom.

"I guess so, but sometimes it feels like no one understands me, that is all. I really want to talk Mommy, but **the words just will not come out.** It makes me sad" said Katie.

"This is why we are all trying to help you Honey, we know it is hard to 'get the words out," said Mom.

"Talking with Dr. Elwood and doing many of the things that we do, like going to school early or after school and having lots of friends come over will hopefully help you feel more comfortable," said Mom.

"I do like school Mommy, and I like my friends, it is just hard sometimes," said Katie.

"I know sweetie, I understand. I am super proud of all your efforts Katie.

You are certainly making quite a bit of progress; like when you pointed to the page in the book for Mrs. Ryan. That was very brave of you," said Mom.

"Oh Mommy, I love you! You **do** understand Katie," she whispered as she slowly drifted to sleep.

The end.

About the Author

Elisa Shipon-Blum DO, is the President and Director of the Selective Mutism Anxiety and Related Disorders Treatment Center (SMart Center) located in Jenkintown, Pennsylvania. She is the Founder and Director Emeritus of the Selective Mutism Association (SMA) and a Director of the Selective Mutism Research Institute (SMRI), a foundation established to study Dr. Shipon-Blum's theories and treatment methodologies on Selective Mutism. In addition, Dr Shipon-Blum is Clinical Assistant Professor of Psychology & Family Medicine at the Philadelphia College of Osteopathic Medicine. She is a board-certified physician who specializes in Selective Mutism.

Dr. Shipon-Blum practices in Jenkintown, PA, and has developed the evidenced-based Social Communication Anxiety Treatment® (S-CAT®) from her years studying and researching individuals with Selective Mutism. She consults worldwide with families, treating professionals, and educators, and has helped thousands of children from around the world overcome Selective Mutism. Based on her successful S-CAT® program, Dr. E also created CommuniCamp™, an intensive group treatment program for children with Selective Mutism, social anxiety, and extreme shyness.

Dr. Shipon-Blum lectures throughout the country on the topic of Selective Mutism, performs school evaluations and training for treating professionals, educators, and parents, and is considered one of the world's leading experts in the treatment, research, and understanding of Selective Mutism. She has been a featured expert on national television programs such as 20/20, CNN, Inside Edition, and Good Morning America, as well as other local, national, and international television and radio broadcasts. In addition, she has been featured in TIME Magazine, People Magazine, and has interviewed with newspapers such as the New York Times, Chicago Tribune, Boston Globe, San Diego Tribune, Philadelphia Inquirer, and Palm Beach Post.

Dr. Shipon-Blum is presently involved in multiple collaborative research projects with top researchers and clinicians. In addition to her research she has written numerous articles and books on Selective Mutism and anxiety including 'Easing School Jitters for the Selectively Mute Child,' 'The Ideal Classroom Setting for the Selectively Mute Child,' 'Understanding Katie,' 'Supplement Treatment Guide Book to Understanding Katie', 'Selective Mutism Summer Vacation & Back to School Guide' and ' Selective Mutism and Social Anxiety Disorder in School .' She has also produced numerous DVDs on the topics of treatment and assessment of Selective Mutism, and the development of school accommodations and interventions for mute children.

Dr. Shipon-Blum (or Dr. E as her patients refer to her) prides herself on being 'down to earth' and 'easy to speak to' and resides with her family in the northeast suburbs of Philadelphia, Pennsylvania. Notably, she is also the mother of a child, Sophie, who suffered from and overcame Selective Mutism and is the inspiration for the work she does each day.

www.SelectiveMutismCenter.org
www.CommuniCamp.org
SMartCenter@SelectiveMutismCenter.org
PH: 215-887-5748

Made in the USA
Thornton, CO
10/24/23 21:27:47

ab7ec270-3d13-47cd-86d5-d71f92d69381R01